MacGregor

by John Mackay

LangSyne
PUBLISHING
WRITING *to* REMEMBER

79 Main Street, Newtongrange,
Midlothian EH22 4NA
Tel: 0131 344 0414 Fax: 0845 075 6085
E-mail: info@lang-syne.co.uk
www.langsyneshop.co.uk

Design by Dorothy Meikle
Printed by Printwell Ltd

ISBN 978-1-85217-056-1

MacGregor

SEPT NAMES INCLUDE:

Caird
Comrie
Crowther
Dochart
Fletcher
Gregor
Gregorson
Gregory
Greig
Grigor
Grierson
King
Leckie
MacAdam
Macaree
Maconacie
MacNee
MacGruder
MacNeish
Malloch
Peter
Petrie
White
Whyte

MacGregor

MOTTO:
Royal is my Race

CREST:
A Gold Lion's Head
wearing an antique Crown

PLANT BADGE:
Pine

TERRITORY:
Glen Orchy, Glen Strae, Glen Lochy,
Glendochart, Rannoch, Balquidder,
Loch Lomond, Loch Katrine
and the Trossachs

Chapter one:

The origins of the clan system

by Rennie McOwan

The original Scottish clans of the Highlands and the great families of the Lowlands and Borders were gatherings of families, relatives, allies and neighbours for mutual protection against rivals or invaders.

Scotland experienced invasion from the Vikings, the Romans and English armies from the south. The Norman invasion of what is now England also had an influence on land-holding in Scotland. Some of these invaders stayed on and in time became 'Scottish'.

The word clan derives from the Gaelic language term 'clann', meaning children, and it was first used many centuries ago as communities were formed around tribal lands in glens and mountain fastnesses.

The format of clans changed over the centuries, but at its best the chief and his family held the land on behalf of all, like trustees, and the ordinary clansmen and women believed they had a blood relationship with the founder of their clan.

There were two way duties and obligations. An inadequate chief could be deposed and replaced by someone of greater ability.

Clan people had an immense pride in race. Their relationship with the chief was like adult children to a father and they had a real dignity.

The concept of clanship is very old and a more feudal notion of authority gradually crept in.

Pictland, for instance, was divided into seven principalities ruled by feudal leaders who were the strongest and most charismatic leaders of their particular groups.

By the sixth century the 'British' kingdoms of Strathclyde, Lothian and Celtic Dalriada (Argyll) had emerged and Scotland, as one nation, began to take shape in the time of King Kenneth MacAlpin.

Some chiefs claimed descent from

ancient kings which may not have been accurate in every case.

By the twelfth and thirteenth centuries the clans and families were more strongly brought under the central control of Scottish monarchs.

Lands were awarded and administered more and more under royal favour, yet the power of the area clan chiefs was still very great.

The long wars to ensure Scotland's independence against the expansionist ideas of English monarchs extended the influence of some clans and reduced the lands of others.

Those who supported Scotland's greatest king, Robert the Bruce, were awarded the territories of the families who had opposed his claim to the Scottish throne.

In the Scottish Borders country – the notorious Debatable Lands – the great families built up a ferocious reputation for providing warlike men accustomed to raiding into England and occasionally fighting one another.

Chiefs had the power to dispense justice and to confiscate lands and clan warfare produced a society where martial virtues – courage, hardiness, tenacity – were greatly admired.

Gradually the relationship between the clans and the Crown became strained as Scottish monarchs became more orientated to life in the Lowlands and, on occasion, towards England.

The Highland clans spoke a different language, Gaelic, whereas the language of Lowland Scotland and the court was Scots and in more modern times, English.

Highlanders dressed differently, had different customs, and their wild mountain land sometimes seemed almost foreign to people living in the Lowlands.

It must be emphasised that Gaelic culture was very rich and story-telling, poetry, piping, the clarsach (harp) and other music all flourished and were greatly respected.

Highland culture was different from other parts of Scotland but it was not inferior or less sophisticated.

Central Government, whether in London or Edinburgh, sometimes saw the Gaelic clans as

"The spirit of the clan means much to thousands of people"

a challenge to their authority and some sent expeditions into the Highlands and west to crush the power of the Lords of the Isles.

Nevertheless, when the eighteenth century Jacobite Risings came along the cause of the Stuarts was mainly supported by Highland clans.

The word Jacobite comes from the Latin for James – Jacobus. The Jacobites wanted to restore the exiled Stuarts to the throne of Britain.

The monarchies of Scotland and England became one in 1603 when King James VI of Scotland (1st of England) gained the English throne after Queen Elizabeth died.

The Union of Parliaments of Scotland and England, the Treaty of Union, took place in 1707.

Some Highland clans, of course, and Lowland families opposed the Jacobites and supported the incoming Hanoverians.

After the Jacobite cause finally went down at Culloden in 1746 a kind of ethnic cleansing took place. The power of the chiefs was curtailed. Tartan and the pipes were banned in law.

Many emigrated, some because they

wanted to, some because they were evicted by force. In addition, many Highlanders left for the cities of the south to seek work.

Many of the clan lands became home to sheep and deer shooting estates.

But the warlike traditions of the clans and the great Lowland and Border families lived on, with their descendants fighting bravely for freedom in two world wars.

Remember the men from whence you came, says the Gaelic proverb, and to that could be added the role of many heroic women.

The spirit of the clan, of having roots, whether Highland or Lowland, means much to thousands of people.

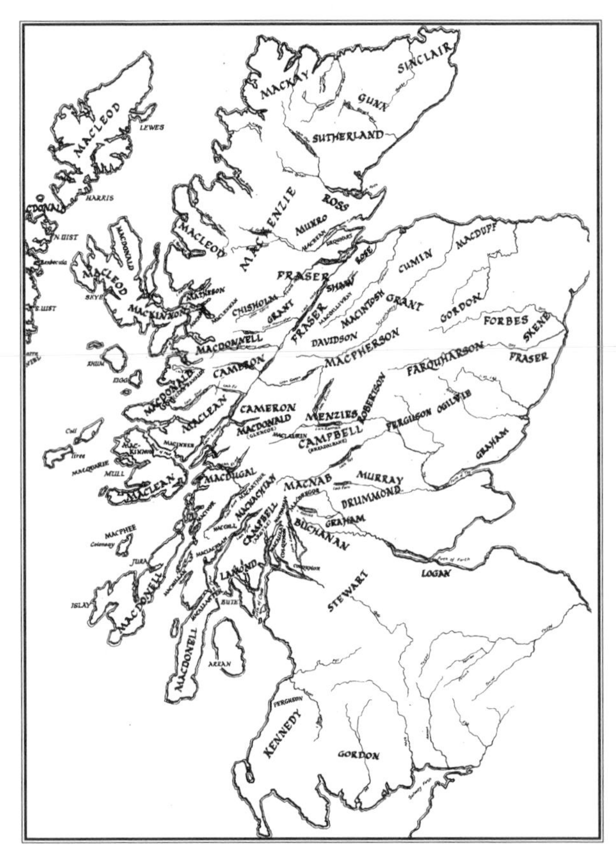

A map of the clans' homelands

Chapter two:

Children of the mist

The MacGregor clan earned the title 'Children of the Mist' in their days of lawlessness when they were most adept of all the clans in vanishing from the scene when it suited them.

The forming of the clan could also be said to be at one with the mists of times remote.

There are claims that the MacGregors were of Pictish origin while other historians have considered them allied to the Celtic tribes who originally came from Europe.

There is a ‘King’ Gregory recorded in ancient script (although ‘king’ could not have meant much more than the leader of a tribe) yet Gregory is surely a clue. That the clan descended from a Gregor, the third son of a King Alpin, is maintained at the end of the eighth century A.D. Then again a ‘Kenneth MacAlpin, the first king of Picts and Scots’ could have prompted the proud MacGregor saying ‘Royal is my race!’

What is agreed from all sources is that while William the Conqueror was landing with his Norman forces at Hastings, the clan MacGregor had come into being and was settled near where Dalmally now occupies a position at the head of Loch Awe; and other lochs to be associated in time with the clan included Loch Vioil, Loch Katrine and Loch Earn.

The family were landowners in Argyll by the end of the 13th century with a John of Glenorchy as their leader and his son Gregor was one of the first recorded instances of the clan name being used.

As the clan’s story developed it was

obvious that they would have a close relationship with their neighbours, the powerful Campbells, alternately being friendly and inter-marrying or feuding to the death.

For instance, Rob Roy's mother was a Campbell and when the clan was made landless and forbidden to use their name, Rob took his mother's name temporarily.

By the middle of the 16th century the MacGregors were spread over a wide area and tending to be 'agin the Government'. They gained a reputation for wildness, particularly around the Rannoch area where their leader went under the colourful title of Duncan the Lordly.

Any Government forces sent into the moorland wastes to deal with these brigands had scant success and the clan went on ever more daring plundering raids.

Despite the fact that they were fellow Roman Catholics, Mary, Queen of Scots, for political reasons decided to continue the persecution of the clan MacGregor.

Much of this harassment had been

enforced by Protestant barons flexing their muscles between the death of Mary's father, James V, and her succeeding to the throne.

In 1563 Mary gave the Campbells of Inveraray the use of royal castles in the Highlands in their campaign to impose law and order and they succeeded in capturing and executing Gregor, the son of Alistair, a prospective chief of the clan and known, because of his skill in archery, as 'the Arrow of Glenlyon'.

The Queen's opposition to the MacGregors was mild (including once, after banishing the clan, reinstating it as a lawful community) in comparison with her son King James VI vindictive war against them.

Persecution of the clan continued after the king went south following the Union of the Crowns for James had his adherents in the Highlands who were ordered to "rout out and exterminate all of that race of malefactors and limmers".

The clan was damned by the king to be lawless and nameless; and women associating with MacGregors were made a public spectacle when stripped naked and whipped through the streets of the nearest townships. Some of the clan fled to Ireland and a choice of surname other than their own had to be made. Death was the penalty against clansmen if more than four people met together; weapons were to be confiscated (the roof thatch was a grand hiding place for the broadsword) and attempts were made to brand the women on the face.

Anyone capturing a MacGregor on producing his head was entitled to that clansman's possessions.

One might wonder how the clan survived. The Scottish Highlands may have had something to do with it. The 'children of the mist' often did not know the meaning of the word surrender but they knew their homeland intimately – the mountain fastnesses, the secret corries, the trackless wastes, as their enemy did not. And the king's orders, sounding so ominous on paper, got no further than that for the less than enthusiastic among his lackeys.

One notable MacGregor who did not escape was Alistair, the victor of the battle of Glen Fruin. He was arrested by a Campbell gang.

On the way to trial, crossing Loch Lomond at night, Alistair vanished overboard and succeeded in swimming to the shore and temporary safety.

Later, influenced by the Duke of Argyll, Alistair agreed to be taken south for an audience with the king and to ask pardon for his Glen Fruin slaughter of the king's men – and the company did actually cross the Border at Berwick.

But a change of purpose set them on a 'U' turn – to Edinburgh where Alistair and relatives who had accompanied him were hanged in the High Street near St. Giles' kirk where eventually a scaffold would be erected to replace the age-old site of execution in the Grassmarket, marked there by a stone design fashioned in the shape of the national flag of Scotland, the St. Andrew's saltire cross, in memory of the Covenanter martyrs who were hanged at this spot.

The opportunity now arose for some of the MacGregor men to join what might be termed a mercenary army and restore some prestige to the clan.

The chance was given them, after King James had gone, by his son Charles I who ordered the Marquis of Montrose to continue the work in attempting to create order in the Highlands and this included opposing the army of Covenanters. Men of the clan agreeing to this would be given 'legal restoration'.

There is no record of how many – if any – volunteered for this mobilisation.

Chapter three:

Rebels with a cause

The persecution through the years had caused the rebel attitude in the clan to become ingrained into their natures.

Callum MacGregor of Glen Fruin was a crack shot and his speciality was in the use of the long-barreled flintlock gun. There is a hillock in Glen Ogle called 'The Knoll of the Dog' where he killed a Campbell bloodhound as it headed a pursuit of him by a Campbell gang, bringing down the beast with a single shot as it leapt over a huge rock where he had hidden himself.

On another occasion, Callum was hiding on an islet on Loch Katrine. The Campbells, grouped on the shore, reckoned that since the islet was bare of sustenance they could starve him out – and settled down to await his surrender.

One of the Campbell men was a cobbler in the rare times of peace and he lit a fire to prepare some food. The smoke rising from the fire silhouetted the figure, making him a good target.

Callum shouted across the water in the Gaelic, "Get out of my sight, you greasy cook!" then shot the man dead.

It happens that in the Gaelic the word 'cook' can also mean 'cobbler'. This uncanny recognition by their quarry of the dim figure by the fire regarding the man's peacetime trade astonished the Campbells; and thinking that Callum must have some personal variation of 'the second sight' – the gift of seeing in the mind's eye a vision of the future – the superstitious Highlanders left the scene and Callum, in his own time, crossed to the mainland shore, homeward bound.

So, into such an uncertain, violent world, Rob Roy MacGregor was born in 1671.

Sir Walter Scott gave this description of the great outlaw as he was in his prime –

'His stature was not of the tallest, but his person was uncommonly strong and compact. The greatest peculiarities of his frame were the breadth of his shoulders, and the great, and almost disproportionate length of his arms; so remarkable

indeed, that it was said he could, without stooping, tie the garters of his Highland hose, which are placed two inches below the knee. His countenance was open, manly, stern at periods of danger but frank and cheerful in his hours of festivity. His hair was dark red, thick, frizzled, and curled short around his face. His fashion of dress showed, of course, the knees and upper part of the leg, which was described to me as resembling that of a Highland bull, hirsute, with red hair and evincing muscular strength similar to that animal. To these personal qualifications must be added a masterly use of the Highland sword, in which his strength of arm gave him great advantage, – and a perfect and intimate knowledge of all the recesses of the wild country in which he harboured, and the character of the various individuals, whether friendly or hostile, with whom he might come into contact.'

In his earlier years he helped farm by the Braes of Balquidder and then became a cattle dealer, sending cattle to the markets in the Lowlands. Life might have gone on in such a comparatively peaceful way for years but one of Rob's business partners vanished, cheating young MacGregor of their joint capital. Luckily Rob had a sum of money entrusted to him by clients, including his being employed in the service of the Duke of Montrose. It happened that, at the time of this misfortune, the cattle trade was suffering a depression. Rob was tempted. With the buy and sell business being at such a low ebb, he began rustling cattle.

When Montrose discovered this, he acted by declaring Rob bankrupt; and made this MacGregor into a rebel by driving Rob's wife and their four young sons from their home in Glengyle. That was the signal for a private war between the Duke and Rob.

The fascination with this most famous outlaw and clansman, who came to be known as 'The Highland Rogue', lies in the contrasts of his living. Where do we fit in the fact that Rob was at one time a member of the Highland Constables? Here is this rebel, this cattle rustler, becoming a policeman, patrolling the mountains! They were organised to prevent Lowland farmers' cattle being stolen by brigands – just like Rob Roy.

Rob's warrior band rose from the surrounding scrub and, with broadswords flashing they came at the Mackintoshes

The farmers paid for this form of protection racket in farm produce but such payment was inclined to lapse when they were not losing their beasts.

That they were nor losing them, Rob would explain, was because of the vigilance of the constables; should they continue to stop paying – often in oatmeal, a staple of the diet at that time, which, because of the circumstances came to be known as 'black meal', hence the derivation of the crime of blackmail – the farmers were reminded they might rue their complacency in the near future.

Another facet of Rob's character was his habit of giving a helping hand to one clan feuding against another. For example, when he was 20, a Strathspey chief of the Grants had quarrelled with his neighbour, a Mackintosh who was diverting a stream for use at his new mill waterwheel thus cutting off the former flow to lower downstream where Grant's mill had ceased to function.

Grant sent word some hundred miles to the south, appealing for help from Rob Roy which in due course was forthcoming.

Sensing trouble, Mackintosh had disposed his men round their mill on guard. Then the Grant men appeared with their chief and accompanied by Rob Roy and his piper. Where, asked Grant, were the MacGregor clansmen? In answer, Rob told his piper to play the stirring 'Rout of Glen Fruin' tune – the signal for Rob's warrior band to rise from the surrounding scrub and, with broadswords flashing they came at the Mackintoshes, driving them off, then set fire to the new mill and thus put a clincher on their day's work.

Rob, in his prime a fighting soldier, could withstand a touch of army discipline, being the only leading member of the clan to join the Earl of Mar in the 1715 Rising, ready to fight for 'The Old Pretender – James III'.

Rob Roy before his death in 1734 had been imprisoned more than once but had always contrived to escape. His last spell away from his native land he served in Newgate Prison in London, saved from a transportation to the Colonies by a timely pardon and returned to his Highland home. He died eight years later at the age of 63 and was buried in Balquidder kirkyard at the head of Loch Voil.

Rob's wife Mary was not as Sir Walter Scott portrays her in his Waverley novel 'Rob Roy' where she becomes an aggressive 'Helen'. Mary was a gentlewoman in the profoundest sense of the word and her cultured character influenced her man in his more domestic moments.

Her three sons (the fourth, Coll, died in his thirties) all fought for Bonnie Prince Charlie in the '45 Rebellion and were at the forefront of the devastating, early morning charge at the brief battle of Prestonpans and continued with that ill-fated army all the way to Derby and on the retreat back over the border. Fortunately for them, the trio were not at Culloden, having gone further north to challenge the clans there who had not joined the Jacobites and whose services might have made a vital difference to their fortunes.

Later, one of them, James, was 'attainted for high treason' for his part in the Rising but, not being among the ringleaders, was pardoned and allowed to go in peace.

But peace was never amenable to James and he persuaded his brother Robin to do a 'Young Lochinvar' act with a lady of considerable wealth about to marry someone else. She was called Jean and was subsequently abducted (to be fair to Robin there is a hint in the record of the incident that love letters between him and the bride had been previously exchanged).

James was arrested for his part in the escapade and imprisoned in 1750 in Edinburgh Castle. His daughter May disguised in male attire as a cobbler visited her father in his cell along with her mother. While the three were by themselves, James was given the cobbler's disguise and left the castle ahead of them followed by May and her mother, a guard not realising a deception had been successfully carried through until he looked in the cell later.

Having escaped the castle and after a series of adventures, James managed to get himself to France and joined other exiles in Paris. The 'Auld Alliance' between Scotland and France caused him to be treated well, beginning a new life until his death there in 1789.

Robin was less fortunate. He was tried for the abduction and condemned to death.

At his execution place in Edinburgh's Grassmarket "he was very genteely dressed and declared he died an unworthy member of the Church of Rome". The severity of the sentence was enforced by the law of that time against him for his upholding of the Jacobite cause. (In the case of another abduction trial of a local baillie's son, the culprit was merely fined £20.)

May, as mentioned above in James's escape from the castle, was also present when her uncle was hanged; and when the hangman was about to divest Robin of his outer finery after the execution had taken place, she fetched the executioner such a clout as sent him sprawling across the causeway surrounding the sccaffold, an action much approved by the Edinburgh mob who always enjoyed a hanging but nursed a hatred of all hangmen.

In the aftermath of Culloden came the

'Abolition and Proscription of the Highland Dress' in the following Act of 1746 by the Government of George II –

'That from and after the first day of August, one thousand, seven hundred and forty seven, no man or boy within that part of Great Britain called Scotland, other as such as shall be employed as Officers and Soldiers in his Majesty's Forces, shall, on any pretext whatever, wear or put on the clothes (that is to say) the Plaid, Philabeg, or little kilt, Trowse, Shoulder-belts, or any part whatever of what peculiarly belongs to the Highland garb; and that no tartan or party coloured plaid or stuff shall be used for Great Coats or upper coats, and if any person shall presume after the said first day of August to wear or put on the aforesaid garments or any part of them, every such person so offending shall be liable to be transported to any of His Majesty's plantations beyond the seas, there to remain for the space of seven years.'

Sometime later two trial regiments were effectively formed to find how effective the

Highlander would respond to military discipline. It was decided that such forces would be intended to take part in the Colonial wars in America, fully armed and with artillery, so that at least they would be posted far away.

Royal pardons had been given to some of the clans some years before but not until 1774 was the Gregor name restored.

The end of an era had come to the Highlands by then. No longer did those remote glens so beloved by the rebel MacGregors have a significance as formerly. Roads were being constructed into these wild places. The clan system faded as 'civilisation' marched north.

However, in George III's time in 1782 came the Repeal of the Act forbidding the wearing of the Highland dress, prompting a renewal of Highland self esteem, boosted some 50 years later by Queen Victoria's regard for Scotland – a regard extending across the Atlantic where descendants of those who had emigrated long ago, hold kilted Highland Games and Gatherings that surely now outnumber those held in their native land.